The Working-With-Science Series

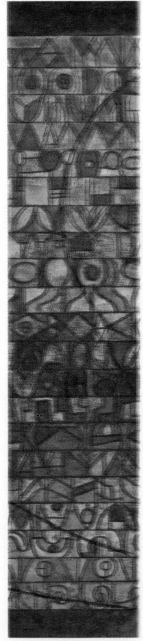

WORKING WITH magnets

E. A. Catherall, B. Sc.
P. N. Holt, B. Sc.

Illustrated by Nicholas Quilliam

ALBERT WHITMAN & Company • Chicago

MATERIALS FOR ACTIVITIES IN THIS BOOK

bar magnets
bell wire, 20 gauge
bowl (not metal)
cardboard
cork
dry cell, 1½ volts
flashlight bulb, 1½ volts
glass jar
globe
horseshoe magnet
  with keeper
iron filings
iron nail
magnetic compass
map
matchbox

metal strip
modeling clay
needle
paper
pin
plastic
ruler
screwdriver
socket for bulb
steel knitting needle
steel screws
styrofoam ball
tacks
thread
water
wood block

Standard Book Number 8075-9226-9
Library of Congress Card Number 68-9117
First published in Great Britain in 1964
by Bailey Bros & Swinfen Ltd
Copyright © 1962 by P. N. HOLT and E. A. CATHERALL
First published in the United States by
Albert Whitman & Company
1969

Cover illustration courtesy of Cornell Aeronautical Laboratory, Inc., Buffalo, N. Y.
Original painting for CAL by H. Bliss, Rochester, N. Y.
Cover design by James Bradford Johnson

Seeing what happens

Keeping notes

WORKING WITH SCIENCE

You want to find out why things happen. You can do this by working with science. You can work the way men and women who are scientists do.

1 Tell what you want to find out.
2 Guess what will happen.
3 See what happens by using real things.
4 Write down what happened.
5 Tell what happened. Is it what you thought would happen? If it is not, what do you think will happen if you begin again? This is how you learn!

Measuring

Thinking why

3

SHAPE AND STRENGTH

1 Have you a magnet? What shape is it? Can you draw it?

2 There are pictures of magnets on page 5. Which magnet is like yours?

3 Have you seen magnets different from those on page 5?

4 Does your magnet have a keeper? Try to find out why it is called a keeper.

5 What will your magnet pick up? Try to pick up all sorts of things. Make a list of things your magnet will pick up.

6 Make a list of things your magnet will not pick up.

7 Look at the things which your magnet will pick up and write down what they are made of. Will your magnet pick up all kinds of metal?

MANY MAGNETS

Magnets are made in different shapes and many sizes. You may have a *bar magnet* or a *horseshoe magnet*. Or you may have a small round magnet used to hold paper on a metal bulletin board. If your horseshoe magnet has a metal bar across its ends, this is its *keeper*. It is a small bar magnet and helps the horseshoe magnet keep its strength.

Did you find your magnet picks up only metals that are iron or steel? A magnet also picks up two metals you are not likely to have. These are cobalt and nickel.

The first magnets men found were rocklike pieces of iron ore. It is said early Greeks found such stones in a place called Magnesia. The word magnet comes from this name.

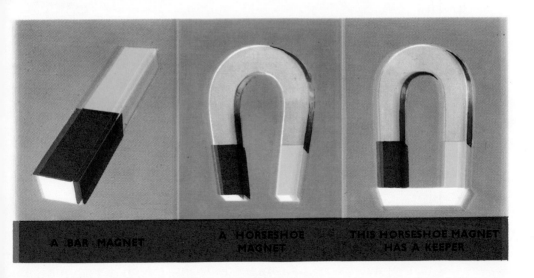

A BAR MAGNET

A HORSESHOE MAGNET

THIS HORSESHOE MAGNET HAS A KEEPER

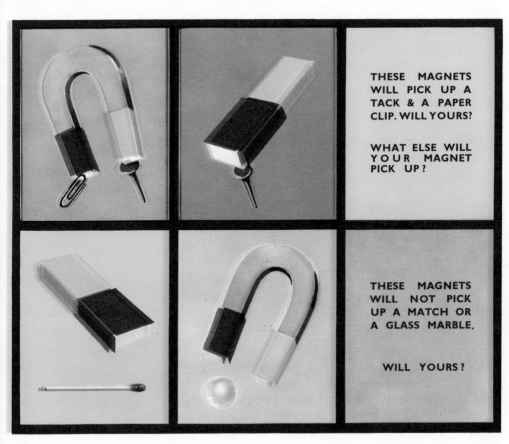

THESE MAGNETS WILL PICK UP A TACK & A PAPER CLIP. WILL YOURS?

WHAT ELSE WILL YOUR MAGNET PICK UP?

THESE MAGNETS WILL NOT PICK UP A MATCH OR A GLASS MARBLE.

WILL YOURS?

TRY THIS WITH YOUR MAGNET

1 Which part of your magnet do you use to pick up things? Will both ends pick up things?

2 Try to pick up things with the middle of the magnet.

3 How many tacks will your magnet pick up?

4 How many tacks can you hang end to end from one place on your magnet?

5 Will the other end hold as many tacks?

6 Draw your magnet with the tacks hanging from it.

7 Place a ruler by your magnet and use a pencil to mark the magnet every half-inch along its length. The picture on page 7 shows a bar magnet marked this way. How many tacks can you hang at each mark on the magnet? Draw your magnet with the tacks.

WHAT YOU FOUND OUT

You know that a magnet pulls, or *attracts*, iron and steel. The ends of your magnet attract more tacks than other parts do. This should make you think your magnet is strongest at its ends. When you try places farther from the ends, the magnet attracts fewer tacks. Its *magnetism* is weaker.

One end of a magnet is just as strong as the other. This is true for both horseshoe and bar magnets.

Your drawing of a magnet attracting tacks at different places will show you a regular pattern. If you shake the tacks off and pick them up again, will you see the same pattern? Yes, you will find the ends always have the strongest attraction. The very center has no attraction, and no tacks are picked up there.

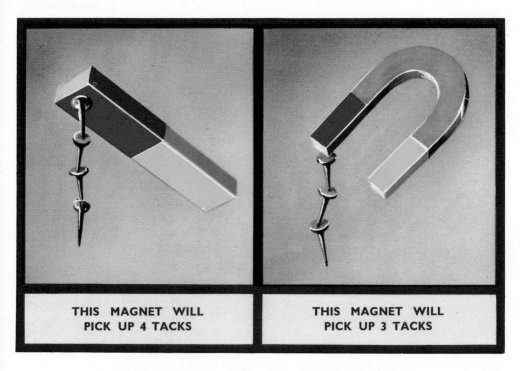

THIS MAGNET WILL
PICK UP 4 TACKS

THIS MAGNET WILL
PICK UP 3 TACKS

WRITE DOWN HOW MANY TACKS YOUR
MAGNET WILL PICK UP. CAN YOU BEAT IT?

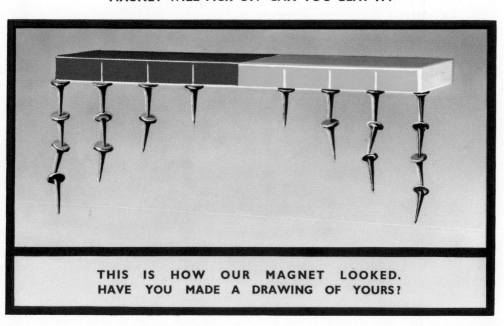

THIS IS HOW OUR MAGNET LOOKED.
HAVE YOU MADE A DRAWING OF YOURS?

SEE WHAT HAPPENS

1 Place a tack on a wooden ruler. Now move your magnet along underneath the ruler. What happens to the tack?

2 How far can you move the tack along the ruler by using your magnet underneath the ruler?

3 Now use the other end of your magnet. Will the end of your magnet pull the tack along the ruler?

4 Will your magnet pull the tack up a sloping ruler? What happens when you take the magnet away?

5 Does your magnet attract through wood? If you could not make your magnet attract the tack through wood, try a thinner piece of wood. What happens?

6 Place a tack in an empty glass jar. Can you lift the tack up the side of the jar by using a magnet outside the jar?

7 What happens when you use the other end of your magnet?

8 Does your magnet attract through glass?

MORE ABOUT MAGNETIC ATTRACTION

By now you have found that a magnet, if it is strong enough, can attract iron or steel through wood and glass.

This may surprise you. Did your magnet attract the wood? Did it attract the glass? No, the magnet could not pull either wood or glass toward itself. But the magnet could attract the steel tack through the wood and through the glass. The *force* that a magnet has is not stopped by wood or glass.

DOES YOUR MAGNET ACT THROUGH THE RULER ?

WILL YOUR MAGNET ACT THROUGH YOUR DESK LID ?
WILL YOUR MAGNET ACT THROUGH A THIN PIECE OF WOOD ?
WILL IT ACT THROUGH A THICK PIECE OF WOOD ?   HOW THICK ?

WILL YOUR MAGNET PULL THE TACK UP A SLOPING RULER ?

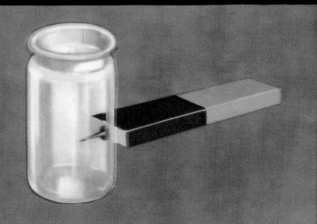

HERE IS OUR TACK CLIMBING UP THE JAM JAR.

HAVE YOU DRAWN YOURS ?

WILL YOUR MAGNET ACT THROUGH A WINDOW PANE ?

WHAT ABOUT OTHER MATERIALS?

1 Put a tack in a glass jar full of water. Hold your magnet in the water. Will the tack jump through the water to get to your magnet?

2 What happens if you use the other end of your magnet?

3 How close does your magnet have to be before the tack is attracted to it?

4 Wrap your magnet in a piece of paper. Will it pick up a tack?

5 Wrap your magnet in plastic. Does your magnet attract a tack through the plastic?

6 Will your magnet act through rubber? Cloth? Nylon? Write down what you try and what you find out.

7 Can you find anything your magnet will not attract through?

THINKING ABOUT WHAT YOU HAVE BEEN DOING

You have found that your magnet can attract a tack through many materials. Glass, wood, water, and plastic will not stop *magnetic force*.

Of course your magnet is only strong enough to attract a tack for a certain distance. Beyond this, it cannot attract the tack, even if only air separates the tack from the magnet.

Did you try attracting a tack through metals? Did aluminum stop the magnetic force? Try dropping the tack in an iron or steel cooking pot. This time your magnet is so attracted to the pot that it does not pull the tack.

WHAT HAPPENED WHEN THE TACK WAS IN THE WATER?

DID YOUR MAGNET PULL THE TACK?

CAN YOU LIFT THE TACK UP THE SIDE OF THE JAR WHEN IT IS FULL OF WATER?

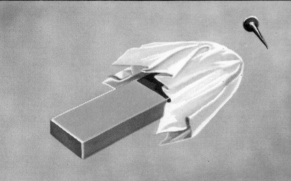

DOES YOUR MAGNET ACT THROUGH PAPER?

WRAP YOUR MAGNET IN A PLASTIC BAG. WILL IT STILL PICK UP A TACK?

WILL YOUR MAGNET ACT THROUGH A TIN BOX?

HOW TO MAKE A MAGNET FOR A SHORT TIME

USE YOUR MAGNET AND LARGE IRON NAILS

1 Try to pick up a tack with an iron nail. Will it attract the tack and lift it up?

2 Now put the head of one nail to the end of your magnet. Hold the magnet and nail above a tack. Will the nail pull the tack up? Write what happens.

3 Take a second nail and hold it above the tack. Quickly touch your magnet to the nail, then pull it away. What happens to the tack?

4 Take a third nail and hold it above a tack. Bring your magnet very slowly toward the head of the nail. Look closely. Does the magnet have to touch the nail before the nail can lift the tack?

SOME THINGS TO WATCH OUT FOR

Your own magnet is a *permanent magnet*. "Permanent" means lasting. A permanent magnet has lasting magnetism.

You found that a nail touched by your permanent magnet acts like a magnet itself. It can pick up a tack. But the nail is not a permanent magnet. It soon loses its magnetism and cannot attract a tack.

Iron nails may keep some magnetism for a short time. This is why it is a good idea to use different nails for the different parts of this activity.

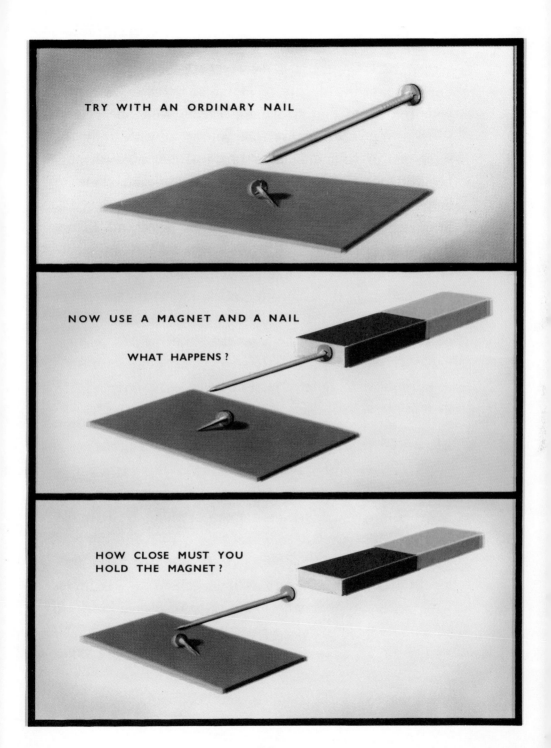

13

ONE WAY TO MAKE A PERMANENT MAGNET
BEGIN WITH A STEEL KNITTING NEEDLE

1 Put the knitting needle on a table. Hold it still with your free hand and stroke the needle with one end of your magnet. Make sure that you are always using the same end of your magnet. Mark one end of your magnet and one end of the knitting needle with chalk to help you do this.

2 Stroke the knitting needle in the same direction. Count the number of strokes. Try 30 strokes. Will your needle pick up tacks? How many? Write down the number.

3 Now make another knitting needle into a magnet. Try 50 strokes. Use this needle to pick up tacks. Will it pick up more tacks than your first knitting-needle magnet did? Which magnet is stronger?

4 A permanent magnet does not have to be large. Look at a *magnetic compass*. The pointer is a magnet.

MORE ABOUT MAGNETISM

You have probably heard that everything is made of *atoms*. We cannot imagine how small atoms are or how many atoms there are in the tiniest thing we can see. But we know that atoms are what make one material different from another.

In the steel knitting needle, each group of atoms acts like a tiny magnet. The groups of atoms are lined up, and one tiny magnet strengthens the next. This makes the whole knitting needle a strong magnet. When you stroked the needle, you used your magnet to pull the atoms into the pattern that made it a permanent magnet.

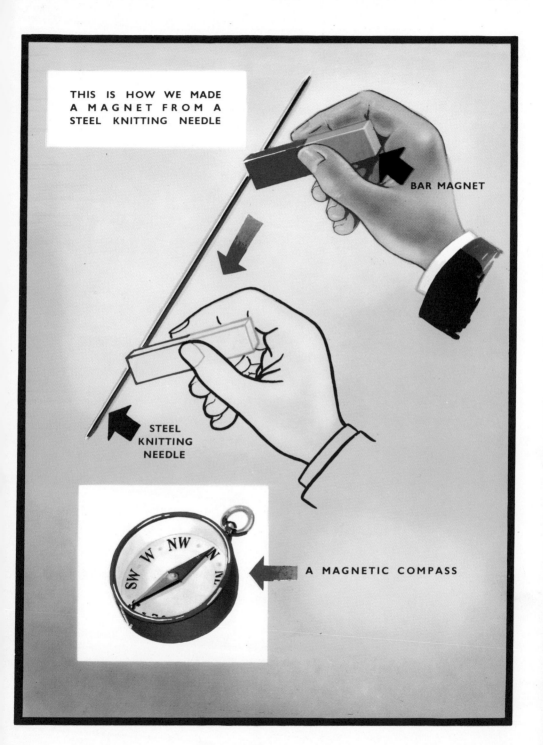

THIS IS HOW WE MADE
A MAGNET FROM A
STEEL KNITTING NEEDLE

BAR MAGNET

STEEL
KNITTING
NEEDLE

A MAGNETIC COMPASS

LET THE COMPASS SHOW YOU

1   Find a magnetic compass. Are the ends of the compass needle, or pointer, different colors? When you put the compass down, which end points North? This is the *north-seeking pole* of the compass needle.

2   Hold something of iron or steel near the compass. Does the needle swing around from north to follow the object? If you take the object away, does the compass again point to the north?

3   Take a knitting needle that is not a magnet. Put your compass at one end, as shown at the top of page 17. Make a drawing to show what happens. Is the same pole of the compass needle attracted to both ends of the knitting needle?

4   Now what happens when you hold the compass near the knitting needle you magnetized? Is it what you see in the lower picture on page 17?

A MAGNET HAS TWO POLES

We have been talking about magnets having two ends. One end is a north-seeking, or north, *pole*; the other is a south pole.

Both the north and the south pole of a magnet will attract or be pulled toward anything made of iron, steel, cobalt, or nickel.

If you have a horseshoe magnet, you can check it with your compass. You will find that it, too, has a north pole and a south pole. It is really a bar magnet that has been bent into the shape of a U.

COMPASS

STEEL KNITTING NEEDLE

THIS IS WHAT HAPPENED WHEN WE HELD OUR COMPASS NEAR A STEEL KNITTING NEEDLE.
WHICH END OF THE COMPASS NEEDLE POINTS TOWARDS THE STEEL KNITTING NEEDLE ?

NEEDLE
MAGNET

WHAT HAPPENED WHEN YOU HELD YOUR COMPASS NEAR ONE END OF YOUR KNITTING NEEDLE MAGNET ?
TRY PUTTING YOUR COMPASS AT THE OTHER END OF YOUR MAGNET WRITE DOWN WHAT HAPPENS.

CAN YOU MAKE YOUR MAGNET LOSE ITS STRENGTH?

1 Test your knitting-needle magnet. How many tacks will it pick up? Bang your needle 10 times on the edge of a table. How many tacks will it pick up now?

2 Magnetize another knitting needle. How many tacks will it pick up? Hold the needle with tongs over a flame. Let it cool. How many tacks will it pick up now?

You found both striking and heating weaken magnetism. This is because a blow or heat throws the atoms out of the order that made the needle a magnet.

17

WILL IT REALLY POINT NORTH?

1 Make a paper sling to hold a bar magnet. (Use the picture on page 19 to help you.) Place the magnet in the sling and put thread through the holes.

2 Hold your magnet up by the thread. Which way does the magnet point? Move it slightly. What happens? Hang the thread from a hook or a chair back so that it can swing freely. Hang it where there is no metal near it. Does the magnet always point the same way?

3 Mark the end of the magnet which is pointing to the North with a letter N. (Use your compass to find North.) This end of the magnet is the north-seeking pole. Mark the other end of the magnet with a letter S. This is the south pole of your magnet.

WHO FIRST USED A COMPASS?

Later in this book you will find out why a free-swinging magnet seeks a north-south position.

Long ago, before anyone could tell why this happened, men used magnets they called *lodestones* to find directions. The name "lodestone" meant "leading stone." The magnet was used to lead the way.

The early Greeks found lodestones, or magnetized pieces of iron ore. So did the Chinese and many other people. No one knows for sure who really invented the first compass. We do know, however, that compasses of different kinds have been used for a thousand years or so.

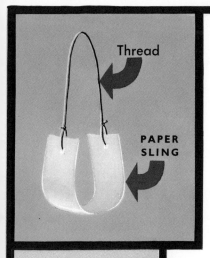

Thread

PAPER SLING

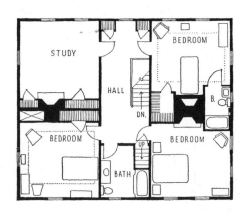

SECOND FLOOR

SUPPOSE YOU MOVE YOUR MAGNET FROM ONE ROOM TO ANOTHER. DOES THIS MAKE ANY DIFFERENCE IN THE WAY YOUR MAGNET POINTS?

MAKE A FLOOR PLAN OF YOUR ROOM.
USE YOUR HOMEMADE COMPASS TO FIND NORTH.
MARK THE DIRECTIONS ON YOUR FLOOR PLAN.

THIS IS HOW WE MARKED OUR MAGNET.

WHICH IS THE <u>NORTH SEEKING</u> POLE OF YOUR MAGNET ?

WHEN YOU BRING TWO MAGNETS TOGETHER

USE TWO BAR MAGNETS

1 Keep your compass magnet hanging in its paper sling. Find a second bar magnet. Bring the south-seeking pole (the south pole) of the magnet in your hand close to the north-seeking (north pole) of your compass magnet. What happens? Does the north pole of one magnet attract or push away the south pole of another magnet?

2 Now bring the north pole of the magnet in your hand close to the north pole of your compass magnet. What happens? Does the north pole of one magnet attract or push away the north pole of another magnet?

TELLING WHAT HAPPENS

You have used *attract* to tell how a magnet pulls iron or steel to itself. When you placed the north pole of one magnet near the south pole of another, you found the poles strongly attracted to each other.

But when you brought two north poles or two south poles together, it was different. Instead of attracting each other, the poles pushed apart. Your hanging compass magnet turned aside just as if you had pushed it with your finger. We say that two poles that are alike *repel*—or push away—each other. A short way to remember what happens is to say that like poles repel, unlike poles attract.

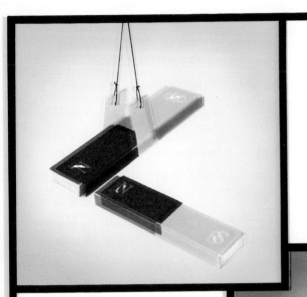

WHAT HAPPENS WHEN YOU PLACE THE NORTH-SEEKING POLE OF ANOTHER MAGNET CLOSE TO THE NORTH-SEEKING POLE OF YOUR COMPASS MAGNET?

DO THEY ATTRACT OR REPEL EACH OTHER?

WHAT HAPPENS WHEN YOU PLACE THE SOUTH POLES OF TWO MAGNETS CLOSE TOGETHER?

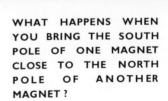

WHAT HAPPENS WHEN YOU BRING THE SOUTH POLE OF ONE MAGNET CLOSE TO THE NORTH POLE OF ANOTHER MAGNET?

DO THEY ATTRACT OR REPEL EACH OTHER?

WILL IT POINT NORTH?

1 As you make this compass, use the pictures on page 23. You will need a cork, a large sewing needle, and a pin. You will also need a bowl and water.

2 Put the pin in the cork and float the cork in the water. The cork should float evenly and turn easily.

3 Magnetize the needle. (Turn back to page 15.) Place the needle on the cork floating in the water. If you wish, drop a little white glue on the needle to hold it on the cork.

4 Watch what the needle and cork do. Does the cork turn on the pivot, then stop? Is the needle in a north-south position? Use the compass you have had for other experiments to check.

5 Try steering a boat by remote control. Make a small boat of wood. Put your magnetized needle on it and then bring a magnet near the boat, as you see on page 23. What happens to the boat? How can you make it turn around? Of course if you used a steel bowl, your boat would cling to the side because of the magnetized needle. Us a glass, plastic, or china bowl.

USING A COMPASS TO TELL DIRECTIONS

Look at the round magnetic compass you have been using. The letter N stands for north, S for south, E for east, and W for west. Turn your compass until the N is under the pointer when it is at rest. Face north. Then east is on your right, west on your left, and south to your back.

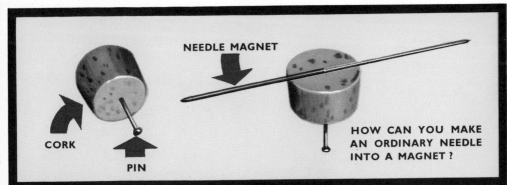

NEEDLE MAGNET

CORK

PIN

HOW CAN YOU MAKE
AN ORDINARY NEEDLE
INTO A MAGNET?

THIS IS HOW OUR
COMPASS LOOKED.

WE USED A
PLASTIC BOWL.

WHY MUST WE NOT
USE A METAL BOWL?

NEEDLE
MAGNET

MAGNET

YOUR BOAT

WORK AND PLAY

1 Magnets are part of many toys and games. Look at some of your own games and see if a magnet is needed.

2 You can have fun with a homemade fish pond. Use a horseshoe magnet tied to a pole for a fishing rod. Cut out fish from heavy paper and slip a paper clip on each fish. Drop your fish in a bowl of water. It isn't as easy to catch the fish as it looks!

3 Look for magnets used in your home. You may have a bulletin board with a thin metal surface. Small magnets hold papers in place on the board. No tacks are needed.

4 Magnets are used to hold doors closed. You will often find magnetic catches on kitchen cabinets.

5 Magnets are often used to hold hooks or clips to metal surfaces. A long magnet fastened on a kitchen wall makes a good knifeholder.

6 Make a list of places where magnets are used in your home. You can add to your list as you go on with this book.

TINY BUT STRONG

Can you believe that a magnet weighing only one pound can hold up 49 pounds? Small but very strong magnets are made from an *alloy* of iron, nickel, aluminum, and one other metal, usually cobalt or copper. (An alloy is a substance made from two or more metals.) *Alnico* is the name given to this alloy which makes very strong permanent magnets.

24

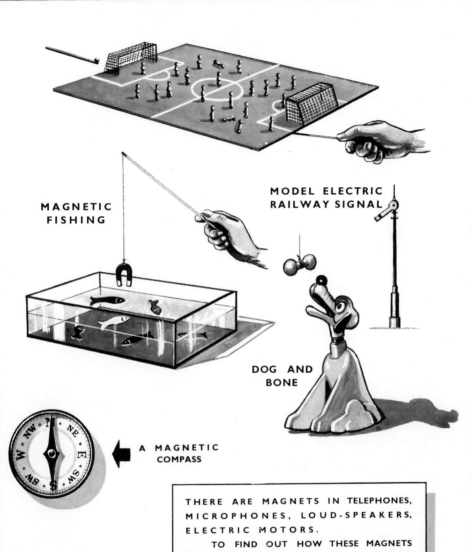

MAGNETIC
FISHING

MODEL ELECTRIC
RAILWAY SIGNAL

DOG AND
BONE

A MAGNETIC
COMPASS

THERE ARE MAGNETS IN TELEPHONES,
MICROPHONES, LOUD-SPEAKERS,
ELECTRIC MOTORS.

TO FIND OUT HOW THESE MAGNETS
WORK, YOU WILL HAVE TO WATCH
CAREFULLY, ASK PEOPLE QUESTIONS,
AND LOOK IN BOOKS, TO FIND SOME
OF THE ANSWERS.

HOW MANY DIFFERENT USES FOR MAGNETS CAN YOU DISCOVER?

THINK ABOUT WHAT YOU SEE

1 Put a magnetic compass on a table. Find the north, south, east, and west.

2 Bring a bar magnet towards your compass from the east. What happens? Remember that unlike poles attract each other. Is the north pole of the compass pulled over to the east by your magnet? Then what pole of your magnet is near the compass? Yes, it is the south pole. But perhaps it was the south pole of your compass that swung over to the pole of your magnet. Then you know that it is the north pole of your magnet (as shown in the picture on page 27) near the compass.

3 Do this experiment again. This time bring your magnet towards the compass from the west. Write down what happens. Does the north pole of your magnet pull the south pole of the compass to the west?

4 How near does your magnet have to be to move your compass needle? Measure the distance with a ruler.

WHICH POLE IS WHICH?

You have worked enough with magnets now to know that there is some force around them that attracts or repels. In the next pages you will learn more about this. You can get ready for new activities by marking which pole of your magnet is which. Use your magnetic compass to find the south pole of your magnet. Mark it with an S in paint, crayon, or chalk. The other pole should be marked with an N.

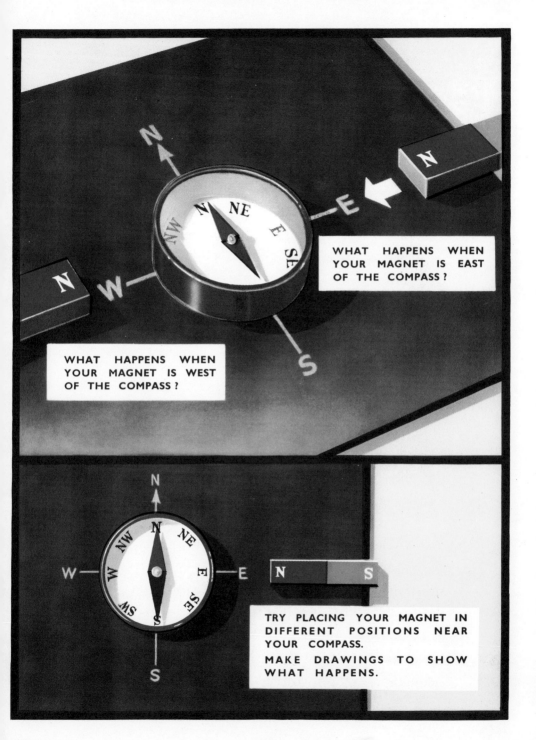

WHAT HAPPENS WHEN YOUR MAGNET IS EAST OF THE COMPASS?

WHAT HAPPENS WHEN YOUR MAGNET IS WEST OF THE COMPASS?

TRY PLACING YOUR MAGNET IN DIFFERENT POSITIONS NEAR YOUR COMPASS.

MAKE DRAWINGS TO SHOW WHAT HAPPENS.

SEEING FOR YOURSELF

1 Place two books side by side with a bar magnet between them. Place a thin piece of cardboard over the books and magnet, as shown on page 29. Sprinkle iron filings on the card. Now tap the card gently.

2 What happens to the iron filings? Draw the pattern the filings make.

3 Where are the lines of your pattern closest together?

4 Now see what pattern you can make using a horseshoe magnet.

5 What happens if you use two bar magnets, side by side with both N poles at one end and both S poles at the other end, as shown on page 29?

WHAT YOU SAW

Each iron filing is a tiny bar of iron. And each filing is attracted to your magnet. If you hold your magnet over a pile of filings, you'll see them jump to the ends of the magnet and cling there. Most of the filings will be at the ends, some on the sides, and none in the middle of the magnet.

When you sprinkle the filings on the cardboard, you keep them from clinging to the magnet itself. The filings show the *magnetic lines of force* around your magnet. See how the lines connect the poles of the magnet. More lines of force are seen at the ends of the magnet than at the sides. This shows the ends, or poles, have the strongest magnetic force.

THIS IS HOW WE DID IT . . . . . .

WE SPRINKLED IRON FILINGS

IRON FILINGS

TAP THE CARD

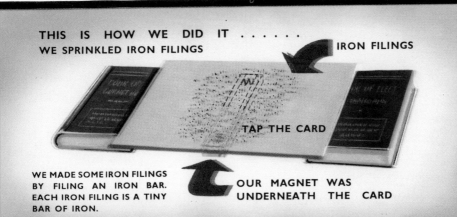

WE MADE SOME IRON FILINGS
BY FILING AN IRON BAR.
EACH IRON FILING IS A TINY
BAR OF IRON.

OUR MAGNET WAS
UNDERNEATH THE CARD

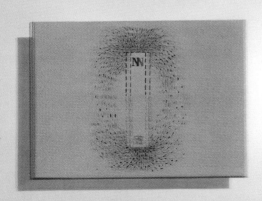

. . . . AND THIS WAS
THE PATTERN WE MADE

HAVE YOU DRAWN
YOUR PATTERN?

WE TRIED PLACING TWO MAGNETS WITH THEIR
NORTH POLES SIDE BY SIDE

DRAW THE PATTERN YOU OBTAINED

SEEING FOR YOURSELF

1   See what other patterns iron filings show when you place magnets in different ways under the cardboard. Try the pattern shown at the top of page 31.

2   Try the magnets as placed in the middle picture. Where do the iron filings show the lines of force are now? How have they changed?

3   Now use only one magnet. Sprinkle the iron filings on the cardboard above the magnet. Place a magnetic compass on the cardboard. Which way does the needle point? Move the compass to another place on the cardboard. Which way does the needle point?

4   Look at the lines of force shown by the iron filings. Can you see anything alike about the way the needle of the compass moves and the lines of force shown by the filings?

A MAGNETIC FIELD

The cardboard shows you a flat picture of the lines of force around a magnet. But there are lines of force on all sides of the magnet. These lines make the *magnetic field* of the magnet.

When two magnets are put side by side, N poles at the same end, they act like one larger, stronger magnet. They have a stronger magnetic field around them.

When you hold your compass in the magnetic field around a magnet, the compass needle swings to follow the lines of force.

WITH THE NORTH AND SOUTH POLES
OF THE MAGNETS SIDE BY SIDE.

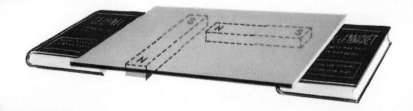

WITH THE MAGNETS IN DIFFERENT POSITIONS.

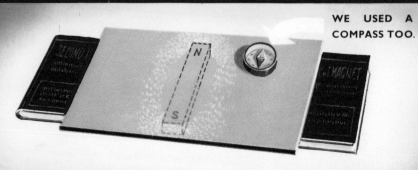

WE USED A
COMPASS TOO.

WHICH WAY DOES YOUR COMPASS NEEDLE POINT?
PLACE YOUR COMPASS IN DIFFERENT POSITIONS.

WHAT YOU WILL NEED

1 We are going to use electricity from a *dry cell,* or *battery.* Chemical action makes this electricity. You can do the activities in this book in many ways, but we shall show you easy ones. Read before you work.

2 You need a 1½ volt dry cell, a 1½ volt flashlight bulb, a socket for the bulb, and number 20 gauge bell wire. You can buy a switch or make one.

3 Find the two posts, or *terminals,* on top of the dry cell. When a wire goes from one terminal to the other, electricity flows along the path. There is an *electric circuit.* Do not make this circuit now.

4 A *switch* turns on and off the *electric current.* When the switch in a circuit is open, no electricity flows. When the switch is closed, then electricity can flow. You can make a switch from a wood block, two flat-headed steel screws, and a strip of metal from a can, any small flat metal bar, or aluminum foil from a frozen food tray folded over and over and flattened.

WARNING

Electricity from a 1½ volt dry cell is safe. NEVER USE HOUSE CURRENT. Use direct current from a dry cell or battery for all the activities in this book.

A dry cell will soon be dead if you connect the terminals with one wire for more than a second at a time. The wire gets dangerously hot. You must have a switch. Always put a light bulb in your circuit. If a circuit without a bulb is needed for an experiment, use a wire 4 feet long and close the switch for a second.

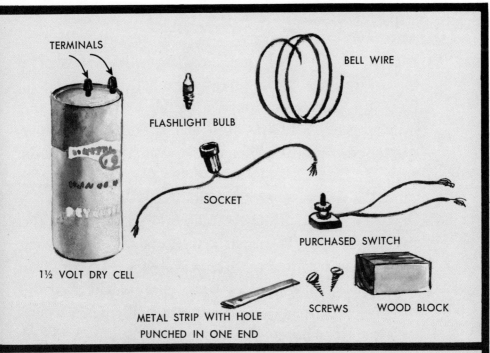

TERMINALS

FLASHLIGHT BULB

BELL WIRE

SOCKET

PURCHASED SWITCH

1½ VOLT DRY CELL

METAL STRIP WITH HOLE
PUNCHED IN ONE END

SCREWS

WOOD BLOCK

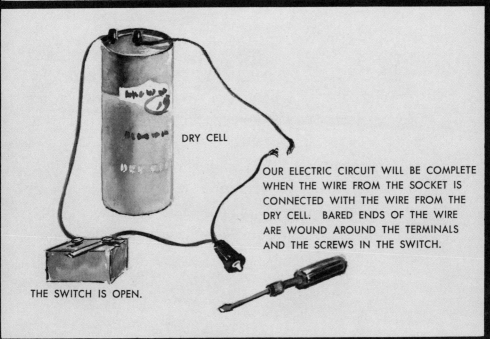

DRY CELL

OUR ELECTRIC CIRCUIT WILL BE COMPLETE
WHEN THE WIRE FROM THE SOCKET IS
CONNECTED WITH THE WIRE FROM THE
DRY CELL. BARED ENDS OF THE WIRE
ARE WOUND AROUND THE TERMINALS
AND THE SCREWS IN THE SWITCH.

THE SWITCH IS OPEN.

WATCHING FOR CHANGES

1 Pull the covering, or *insulation,* from both ends of a wire. Wrap one end around a terminal of the dry cell. Wrap the other end around a switch screw. Keep the switch open. Wire the bulb and socket to the other terminal of the dry cell and the switch, as shown on page 33. Does the bulb light? Why not?

2 Close the switch. Does the bulb light? Why?

3 Open the switch. Take the bulb and socket out of the circuit. Connect the switch to the terminals. Place your compass on top of one wire, as on page 35.

4 Watch the compass needle while you quickly close the switch, then open it. What happens? Try again—does the same thing happen? Do not leave the switch closed long enough to let your wires get hot. It uses up electricity too fast.

WHEN ELECTRIC CURRENT FLOWS THROUGH A WIRE

When the bulb lighted as you closed the switch it proved electricity was flowing through the circuit made with the wire and dry cell.

The compass needle moves when electricity flows through a wire. Remember how the compass moved when you held it in the magnetic field around a permanent magnet. A wire carrying electricity is like a magnet. It has a magnetic field.

OUR CIRCUIT IS COMPLETE.

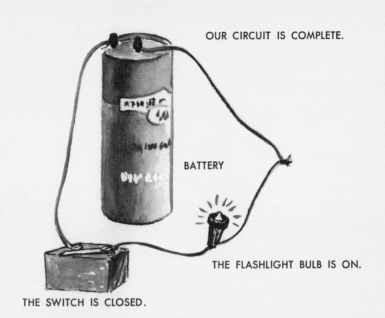

BATTERY

THE FLASHLIGHT BULB IS ON.

THE SWITCH IS CLOSED.

CLOSE AND OPEN THE SWITCH QUICKLY.
WHAT DOES THE COMPASS NEEDLE DO?

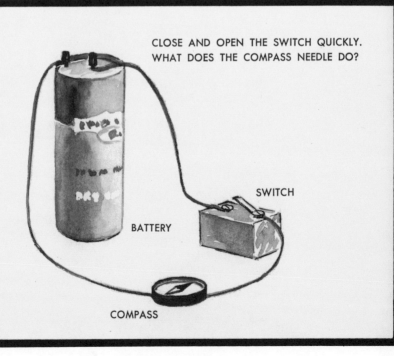

SWITCH

BATTERY

COMPASS

MORE CHANGES TO WATCH FOR

1   Connect the terminals of your dry cell and your switch to make a circuit. Place the compass on the wire. This is shown at the bottom of page 35. Close the switch quickly. See in which direction the north pole of your compass points.

2   Now connect the two wires to the opposite terminals, as shown at the top of page 37. Close the switch. Look at the compass needle. Has it reversed its position, that is, does it point in the opposite direction?

3   See if you can use your compass to tell when current flows in your circuit. Hide the switch behind a book. Get a friend to switch the current on and off. Can you tell when the current is switched on or off by watching the compass needle?

MORE ABOUT THE MAGNETIC FIELD AROUND A WIRE

You saw the compass needle reverse itself when you reversed the wires to the dry cell terminals. The needle reversed its position because the current was reversed and flowed in the opposite direction.

When your switch was hidden, you could use your compass to tell, or *detect*, when the current flowed. The magnetic field around the wire made the compass needle move when electricity flowed.

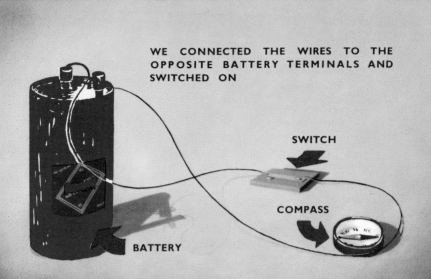

WE CONNECTED THE WIRES TO THE OPPOSITE BATTERY TERMINALS AND SWITCHED ON

SWITCH

COMPASS

BATTERY

WHAT HAPPENS TO THE COMPASS NEEDLE ?

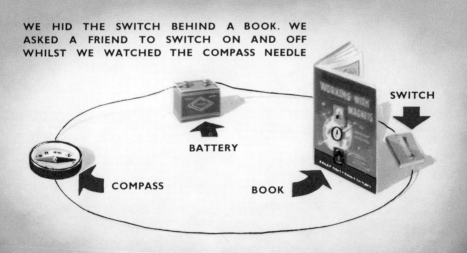

WE HID THE SWITCH BEHIND A BOOK. WE ASKED A FRIEND TO SWITCH ON AND OFF WHILST WE WATCHED THE COMPASS NEEDLE

SWITCH

BATTERY

COMPASS

BOOK

TRY THIS . . . . . HOW MANY TIMES DO YOU GET THE RIGHT ANSWER ?

MAKING A DETECTOR

1 Place your compass in a small box. Wind your wire one turn around the box and connect the wire to the open switch and dry cell. Close the switch for a second. Write down what happened to the compass needle.

2 Now wind another wire ten times around the box with the compass in it. Connect your circuit and close your switch for a second. Write down what happens to the compass needle. Does the needle move more quickly and as if the force was stronger when there are ten turns of wire around the box instead of only one turn?

A FAMOUS EXPERIMENT

Your compass with the wire around it makes a simple *detector* for direct electric current. The more turns of wire, the quicker and stronger the compass needle moves. Many turns of the wire around the compass make it possible to detect a very weak direct current.

Did you notice that the compass moved to a position exactly across, or at right angles to, the wire when the current flowed? The poles of the compass reversed position when the flow of electricity was reversed (as you saw on pages 36-37).

The first experiment with a compass and current was done 150 years ago by Hans Christian Oersted. He lived and worked in Denmark and was famous for his work with electricity and magnetism.

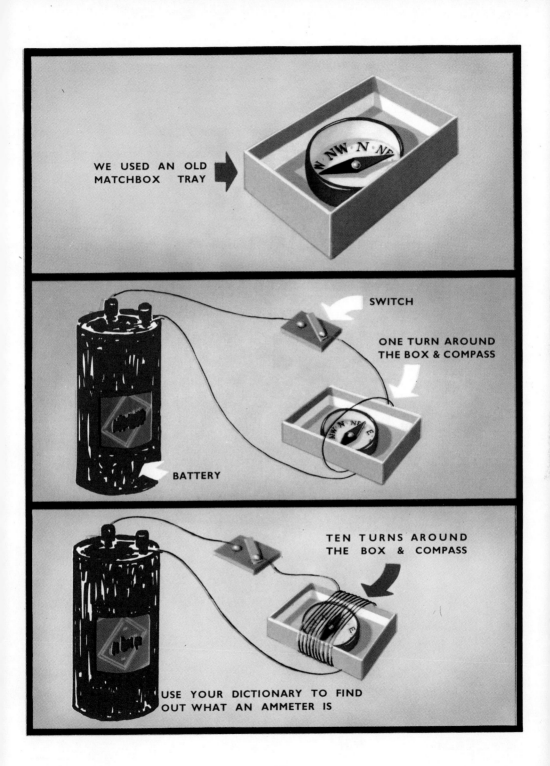

WE USED AN OLD MATCHBOX TRAY

SWITCH

ONE TURN AROUND THE BOX & COMPASS

BATTERY

TEN TURNS AROUND THE BOX & COMPASS

USE YOUR DICTIONARY TO FIND OUT WHAT AN AMMETER IS

YOUR ELECTROMAGNET CAN DO WORK

1 You will need insulated bell wire about 6 feet long, like the kind you have been using, a large iron nail or bolt, a switch, and a dry cell.

2 Make sure that the nail is not magnetized. How can you make sure? Try picking up some tacks or iron filings with the nail. If the nail or bolt picks up the tacks, what do you know about it?

3 Wind your piece of wire 20 times around the nail. Connect your circuit and close the switch. Try to pick up tacks with the nail. How many will it pick up? You have made an *electromagnet*.

4 Don't let the electric current flow long. Open the switch. What happens to the tacks when you stop the electric current flowing from the battery?

5 Now wind the wire 40 times around the nail, always winding in the same direction. How many tacks will your electromagnet pick up this time? Is it more tacks or fewer than you could pick up before?

USEFUL ELECTROMAGNETS

Electromagnets have many uses because their magnetism can be turned on and off. Perhaps you have seen a huge electromagnet hung from a real crane and used to pick up scrap iron and steel.

You may know that your telephone, your doorbell, a magnetic tape recorder, and a hi-fi speaker all make use of electromagnets.

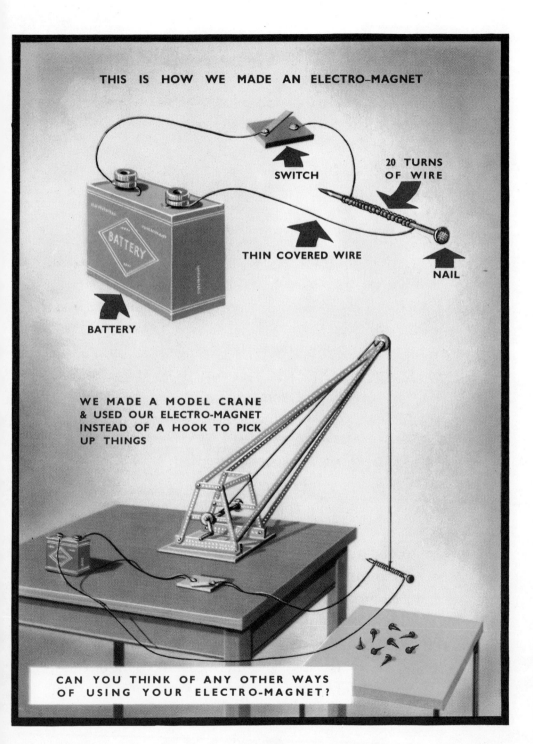

THIS IS HOW WE MADE AN ELECTRO-MAGNET

SWITCH

20 TURNS OF WIRE

THIN COVERED WIRE

NAIL

BATTERY

WE MADE A MODEL CRANE & USED OUR ELECTRO-MAGNET INSTEAD OF A HOOK TO PICK UP THINGS

CAN YOU THINK OF ANY OTHER WAYS OF USING YOUR ELECTRO-MAGNET?

THE EARTH AS A MAGNET

FINDING NORTH

1 Place your magnetic compass on a desk or table. Make sure that it is not near anything made of metal. Which way does the compass needle point?

2 Now find which way the compass needle points when you are outdoors. Try several places, indoors and outdoors. Which way does the compass needle point each time? What do we call this direction?

3 When you are outdoors, draw an arrow on the ground pointing in the same direction as the compass needle. Can you draw in the other points of the compass—east, south, and west?

4 Write down a list of ways of using a compass. Who might use a compass in his work?

5 Do you ever use a compass to guide you when you are hiking? Can you use a compass and a map?

THE EARTH HAS A MAGNETIC FIELD

Do you remember how your compass needle moved when you held your compass in the magnetic field around a bar magnet? Your compass needle points north because the earth has a magnetic field. The compass needle lines up with the magnetic lines of force.

You probably thought of explorers using compasses. You know that sailors and flyers need compasses to stay on their courses. A driver often likes to have a car compass to make sure he is driving in the right direction. Surveyors and mapmakers of all kinds use compasses in their work.

THIS WAS HOW WE FOUND OUR DIRECTIONS

WE MARKED THE DIRECTIONS ON THE CLASS-ROOM FLOOR AND ALSO IN THE PLAYGROUND

HOW CAN YOU MAKE SURE THAT THE MAP IS LYING IN THE RIGHT DIRECTION?

CAN YOU USE A COMPASS & MAP?

IN WHAT DIRECTION DOES YOUR HOUSE FACE?

WHAT IS THE DIRECTION FROM YOUR HOUSE TO YOUR SCHOOL?

IN WHICH DIRECTION DOES THE SUN SET?

LOOK AT A MAP OF YOUR TOWN. IN WHAT DIRECTION DOES THE MAIN STREET NEAREST YOUR HOUSE RUN?

NORTH POLE AND NORTH MAGNETIC POLE

1 Have you a globe of the world in your home or class-room? Look at it carefully. Find the North Pole. This is one end of the line, or axis, around which the earth turns.

2 Look for Bathurst Island. It is in Canada, northwest of the big island called Baffin Island, which is near Greenland. The *north magnetic pole* is near Bathurst Island.

3 Use a styrofoam ball as a model of the earth. Push a plastic knitting needle right through the center. This is the axis and its ends are the North Pole and the South Pole, the earth's *geographic poles.*

4 Magnetize a thin steel knitting needle and push it through the styrofoam ball, as shown on page 45. Now tip your model as you see a globe tipped and push the plastic knitting needle into a block of balsa wood or a large lump of modeling clay.

5 Explore the surface of your model with a small com-pass. In which way does the compass needle always point? If the magnetic field around the steel knitting needle is strong enough, your compass shows north on your model globe.

MORE ABOUT THE MAGNETIC NORTH POLE

The geographic North Pole is an unchanging point. But the magnetic north pole moves from time to time. Scientists do not agree about why this happens, but they can map its location.

HERE IS A CLASSROOM GLOBE.

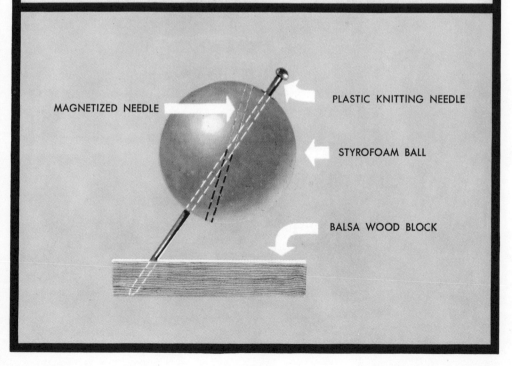

MAGNETIZED NEEDLE

PLASTIC KNITTING NEEDLE

STYROFOAM BALL

BALSA WOOD BLOCK

HOW TO TEST THE STRENGTH OF A MAGNET

SUPPOSE YOU HAVE TWO COMPASSES,
WHICH IS STRONGER?

1 Place a ruler on each side of a magnetic compass so that one is to the east and one is on the west. Use the pictures on page 47 as a guide.

2 Now place a magnet on the east side of the compass and 6 inches away from it. Make the south pole of your magnet point toward the compass.

3 Now place another magnet 6 inches from the compass on the west side. Again make sure that the south pole of this magnet points toward the compass.

4 Is the compass needle still pointing to the north? If it is, your magnets are the same strength. If the magnets are not of the same strength, then the compass needle points toward the stronger magnet.

5 Suppose one magnet is stronger than the other. Try moving the magnets along the rulers until the compass needle points directly north. You have now balanced the pull of your magnets. The magnet that is farther from the compass is the stronger of the two.

MORE ABOUT MAGNETS

This book has helped you find out some things about magnets and magnetism. But you have really just begun. Encyclopedias, science books, and magazines are places where you can learn more about magnets. In some of these you'll see games and tricks you can do with magnets. In others you'll learn some of the new ways magnetism is used in science. It's an exciting story!

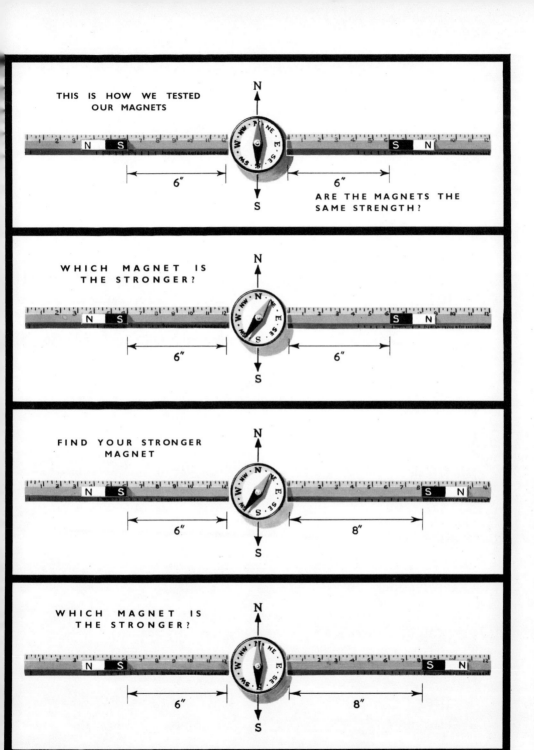

THIS IS HOW WE TESTED OUR MAGNETS

6"

ARE THE MAGNETS THE SAME STRENGTH?

WHICH MAGNET IS THE STRONGER?

6"

6"

FIND YOUR STRONGER MAGNET

6"

8"

WHICH MAGNET IS THE STRONGER?

6"

8"

47

SCIENCE VOCABULARY

You will find an explanation or definition of a word or phrase by turning to the page number given in italics.